THE ULTIMATE GU GOOGLE'S REVOLUTIONARY GEMINI AI

STAYING AHEAD OF THE CURVE

LIAM HENRY JR

The Ultimate Guide to Using Google's Revolutionary Gemini AI: Staying Ahead of the Curve

Table of Contents

Preface

Welcome to the world of AI-powered content creation with Gemini AI! Whether you're a seasoned content creator or just starting out, this book is your guide to unlocking the potential of this revolutionary tool.

In today's content-saturated world, the ability to create high-quality content consistently can feel like a daunting task. Gemini AI steps in as your partner, streamlining workflows, sparking creative ideas, and elevating the quality of your content.

This book is more than just a user manual. We'll delve into the core functionalities of Gemini AI, equip you with advanced techniques to push the boundaries, and explore unforeseen applications that will transform your content creation process.

But Gemini AI isn't meant to replace you. The future of content creation lies in human-AI collaboration. We'll show you how to hone your strategic thinking skills, refine your editing expertise, and maintain your creative spark in this evolving landscape.

By the end of this journey, you'll be a master of Gemini AI, confidently crafting remarkable content that captivates your audience and achieves your content marketing goals. So, get ready to embrace the future of content creation and write your own success story with the power of AI by your side!

Chapter 1

Welcome to the Future of Content Creation with Gemini AI

This chapter sets the stage for your book, introducing readers to the revolutionary world of Gemini AI and its potential to transform content creation.

1.1 What is Gemini AI and Why Should You Care?

The Dawn of a New Era in Content Creation

Welcome to the age of artificial intelligence (AI) in content creation! Buckle up, because Google's Gemini AI is poised to revolutionize the way you approach content generation. But what exactly is Gemini AI, and why should you care?

Meet Your AI Writing Partner: Gemini AI Defined

Imagine a powerful tool that can:

Craft compelling blog posts and articles on demand.

Generate fresh ideas to break through writer's block.

Refine your existing content for clarity and impact.

This is the magic of Gemini AI. Developed by Google's cutting-edge AI research team, Gemini AI utilizes sophisticated algorithms to understand the nuances of human language. It can analyze vast amounts of data, learn writing styles, and even generate creative text formats.

Why Gemini AI Matters: A Content Creator's Dream

Here's why you, as a content creator, should be excited:

Boost Your Productivity: Imagine churning out high-quality content in a fraction of the time. Gemini AI can handle the heavy lifting of content generation, freeing you to focus on strategy and refinement.

Beat the Content Drought: Struggling with writer's block? Gemini AI can provide fresh ideas and spark inspiration, ensuring a steady flow of content.

Stay Ahead of the Curve: The content landscape is constantly evolving. By embracing AI tools like Gemini AI, you demonstrate your commitment to innovation and position yourself for success in the digital age.

Whether you're a seasoned writer, a busy entrepreneur, or just starting your content creation journey, Gemini AI can be your secret weapon. It's more than just a fancy tool; it's a transformative partner that empowers you to create impactful content with unprecedented efficiency.

1.2 Unveiling the Potential of Google's AI Writing Technology

Under the Hood of Gemini AI: How AI Powers Content Creation

In section 1.1, we explored the "what" and "why" of Gemini AI. Now, let's delve deeper and unveil the "how." This section will shed light on the fascinating world of AI writing technology and how Gemini AI leverages it to create powerful content solutions.

Demystifying the AI Magic:

Understanding Machine Learning: Briefly explain how Gemini AI utilizes machine learning algorithms. Mention its ability to analyze massive amounts of text data, including articles, books, and websites. This data allows AI to learn about language structure, grammar, and writing styles.

The Power of Natural Language Processing (NLP): Introduce the concept of NLP and how it empowers Gemini AI. Explain how NLP allows the tool to understand the meaning behind words, analyze context, and even translate languages.

From Data to Content: How Gemini AI Generates Text

Prompt-Based Creation: Explain how Gemini AI relies on user prompts to generate content. Users provide instructions, keywords, or outlines, and the AI uses its knowledge to craft original text.

Content Styles and Tones: Highlight Gemini AI's ability to adapt to different writing styles and tones. This could include formal business writing, casual blog posts, or even creative storytelling formats.

Beyond Text Generation: Expand the discussion by mentioning that Gemini AI can do more than just create new content. It can also assist with editing existing content, suggesting improvements to grammar, clarity, and flow.

A Word on Limitations: Human Expertise Still Reigns Supreme

While AI writing technology is impressive, it's important to acknowledge its limitations. Here's what to keep in mind:

Fact-Checking and Verification: Emphasize that AI-generated content requires human oversight for factual accuracy. Users should verify information and ensure it aligns with their intended message.

The Importance of Creativity: While AI can spark ideas, true creative vision remains a human domain. Users should provide clear direction and leverage AI as a tool to enhance, not replace, their own creativity.

The Future is Now: A Glimpse into Advanced AI Writing

Conclude this section by hinting at the future possibilities of AI writing technology. Briefly mention advancements in areas like sentiment analysis and the ability to generate different creative text formats like poems or scripts. This will pique reader interest and leave them wanting to learn more about the future of Gemini AI.

1.3 Staying Ahead of the Curve: How Gemini AI Can Transform Your Workflow

The content creation landscape is a relentless beast. Deadlines loom, content calendars overflow, and the pressure to stay relevant is ever-present. In this fast-paced environment, embracing innovative tools like Gemini AI can be your key to unlocking a more efficient and productive workflow.

Streamlining Your Content Creation Process:

From Blank Page to Content Bonanza: Gemini AI eliminates the dreaded "blank page" syndrome. By generating drafts or outlines, it kickstarts the content creation process, saving you valuable brainstorming time.

Content Generation on Autopilot: Once you've provided the initial prompt, Gemini AI takes the reins. It can research related topics, generate content based on specific keywords, and even suggest headlines and titles.

Batch Content Creation: The power of Gemini AI lies in its ability to automate repetitive tasks. Imagine generating multiple blog posts, social media captions, or email newsletters in a fraction of the usual time.

Beyond Efficiency: Enhanced Quality and Consistency

Breaking Through Writer's Block: We've all been there - staring at the cursor, devoid of inspiration. Gemini AI can be your creative muse. By offering fresh ideas and different writing styles, it can help you overcome writer's block and keep your content flowing.

Maintaining Consistency: Building a strong brand voice requires consistency. Gemini AI can learn your preferred writing style and tone, ensuring all your content maintains a unified voice across platforms.

Elevating Content Quality: AI excels at grammar and syntax. By leveraging Gemini AI for editing and proofreading, you can ensure your content is polished, error-free, and delivers a professional impact.

The Future of Work: A Collaborative Approach

The rise of AI doesn't signal the end of human content creators. Instead, it fosters a collaborative partnership. By utilizing Gemini AI to handle the heavy lifting, you can free up your time for tasks that require your unique human touch, such as:

Strategic Content Planning: AI can assist with content ideation, but you'll still need your strategic expertise to define content goals and align content with your overall marketing strategy.

Refining the Voice and Message: While AI can maintain consistency, your editorial eye is irreplaceable. You ensure the final content reflects your brand personality and resonates with your target audience.

Adding the Human Touch: Infuse your content with your unique perspective, insights, and experiences. AI cannot replicate the emotional connection and storytelling ability that humans bring to content.

Embrace the Future, Stay Ahead of the Curve

By integrating Gemini AI into your workflow, you can achieve a level of efficiency and content quality that was once unimaginable. Remember, AI is a powerful tool, but it's YOU who holds the reins. As you explore the capabilities of Gemini AI, you unlock an exciting future of content creation – one where you work smarter, not harder, and continuously stay ahead of the curve in the ever-evolving digital landscape.

Chapter 2

Getting Started with Gemini AI: A Step-by-Step Guide

Welcome to the exciting world of Gemini AI! This chapter is your launchpad, guiding you through the setup process and equipping you with the essential skills to navigate the interface and unleash the creative potential of this groundbreaking tool.

2.1 Setting Up Your Gemini AI Account: A Beginner's Guide

Congratulations on taking the first step towards a more efficient and creative content creation process! This section will guide you effortlessly through setting up your Gemini AI account.

Effortless Account Creation:

Locating the Launchpad: Gemini AI is currently under development, and the specific access method might change in the future. Here, we'll explore two common possibilities:

Website Access: If Gemini AI has a dedicated website, simply head to https://blog.google/technology/ai/google-gemini-ai/ in your web browser.

Application Download: If Gemini AI is offered as an application, you'll likely find it on the official Google app store or download page. Search for "Gemini AI" and follow the download and installation instructions for your device.

Sign Up or Sign In Seamlessly:

New Google Account: If you don't have a Google account yet, click the "Sign Up" button and follow the on-screen prompts to create a new account. This will provide you with access to various Google services, including Gemini AI.

Existing Google Account: If you already have a Google account (used for Gmail, YouTube, etc.), click the "Sign In" button and enter your existing Google account credentials. This is the most convenient option if you're already part of the Google ecosystem.

Welcome Aboard!: Once you've successfully signed up or signed in, you'll likely be greeted by a welcome message. This might include a brief introductory video or interactive tutorial to familiarize you with the basic functionalities of Gemini AI. Take some time to explore these resources, as they'll equip you with the foundational knowledge to navigate the platform effectively.

Bonus Tip: Keep an eye out for any verification emails or steps you might need to complete to fully activate your Gemini AI account.

By following these simple steps, you'll be up and running with your Gemini AI account in no time! The next section will delve into mastering the interface and navigating the essential features of this powerful content creation tool.

2.2 Navigating the Interface: Mastering the Essentials

Welcome aboard the Gemini AI spaceship! Now that you've set up your account, it's time to explore the bridge – the user interface, where you'll command this powerful content creation tool. This section will equip you with the knowledge to navigate with confidence and unlock the full potential of Gemini AI.

A Familiarization Tour:

Imagine the Gemini AI interface as your mission control center. Here's a breakdown of the key areas you'll encounter:

Workspace: This is the central hub where the magic happens. It's where you'll interact with Gemini AI by providing prompts, instructions, and reviewing the generated content. Expect a text box or editing area where you can input your requests and see the AI's output.

Prompt Bar: This is your command center! Here, you'll craft clear and concise instructions for Gemini AI. The prompt bar might include options to specify the content type (blog post, email, social media caption), desired tone (formal, casual), and any relevant keywords or themes you want the AI to focus on.

Settings Menu: Think of this as your personalization station. Here, you can fine-tune your Gemini AI experience. You might be able to adjust settings like:

Content Length: Specify the desired length of the generated content, from short snippets to full-length articles.

Writing Style: Choose from a range of writing styles, such as informative, persuasive, or creative, to match the tone of your content.

Output Format: Select the format you prefer for the generated content, such as plain text, HTML, or even a specific content management system (CMS) format for easy integration with your website.

Understanding Workflows (if applicable):

Some versions of Gemini AI might offer pre-defined workflows to streamline your content creation process. These workflows could be designed for specific content types, such as blog posts, social media content, or product descriptions.

Predefined Workflows: If available, explore the pre-defined workflows offered by Gemini AI. Each workflow might guide you through a step-by-step process, prompting you for specific information and generating tailored content based on your selections.

Custom Workflows: In some cases, Gemini AI might allow you to create your own custom workflows. This could be helpful if you have a specific content creation process you want to replicate or automate.

Exploring Additional Features:

The Gemini AI interface might offer additional features to enhance your content creation experience. Be sure to explore these features and see how they can benefit your workflow. Here are some possibilities:

Content History: This feature could allow you to review past interactions with Gemini AI, including prompts, generated content, and any saved projects.

Integration Options: Look for options to integrate Gemini AI with other tools you use, such as grammar checkers, plagiarism detection software, or your content management system.

Help and Support: Having a question or facing an issue? Most interfaces provide easy access to help documentation, tutorials, or a support section where you can find answers and troubleshooting tips.

Remember: The specific layout and features of the Gemini AI interface might evolve over time. However, by understanding these core elements, you'll be well-equipped to navigate any interface and unleash the power of this innovative tool.

By familiarizing yourself with the interface and its functionalities, you'll be well on your way to becoming a master of Gemini AI. The next chapter dives into the heart of the matter – exploring the core functions of Gemini AI and unlocking its content creation potential.

2.3 Customizing Your Preferences: Tailoring Gemini AI to Your Needs

One of the superpowers of Gemini AI lies in its adaptability. This section empowers you to personalize your experience and transform Gemini AI into an extension of your unique content creation style.

Fine-Tuning Your Voice: Defining Your Writing Style

Gemini AI is a chameleon – it can adapt its writing style to match your needs. Here's how to leverage this feature:

A Spectrum of Styles: Imagine a dial allowing you to choose the desired formality of your content. Do you prefer a crisp, professional tone for business reports? Or a more casual, conversational style for blog posts? Gemini AI can generate content that aligns with your preference.

Finding Your Voice: Beyond formality, explore options to define the overall voice and personality you want your content to convey. Do you want it to be friendly and approachable? Authoritative and informative? With clear instructions, Gemini AI can tailor the content to reflect your brand voice.

Humor Me? For some content types, a touch of humor can be engaging. If this aligns with your brand voice, Gemini AI might offer options to generate content with a lighthearted or humorous tone.

Industry Speak: Customization for Specific Fields

The beauty of Gemini AI lies in its potential to understand and cater to specific industries. Here's how to harness this power:

Industry-Specific Terminology: Working in a niche field like finance or healthcare? Provide Gemini AI with relevant keywords and terminology. This will allow the AI to generate content that is not only grammatically correct but also reflects the specific language and jargon used in your industry.

Curated Content: Imagine generating blog posts or articles pre-populated with relevant industry data, statistics, or research. By understanding your field, Gemini AI can curate content that showcases your expertise and establishes you as a thought leader.

Staying on Topic: Some content creation tools can go off on tangents. Gemini AI might offer features to ensure your content stays focused. Provide relevant keywords and thematic constraints to keep the AI on track and generate content that adheres to your specific industry needs.

Building a Bridge: Integrating with Existing Tools

Imagine a seamless workflow where Gemini AI integrates with the tools you already use. Here's how to explore these possibilities:

Exporting for Efficiency: Let's say you generate a fantastic blog post with Gemini AI. Look for options to export the content directly into your content management system (CMS) for easy publishing.

Data Harmony: Do you leverage other content creation tools for tasks like grammar checking or plagiarism detection? Explore if Gemini AI integrates with these tools, allowing you to seamlessly move your content through various stages of the creation process.

API Access (if applicable): For advanced users, some versions of Gemini AI might offer API access. This allows you to connect Gemini AI with custom-built applications or workflows, creating a truly personalized content creation ecosystem.

By tailoring Gemini AI to your preferences and workflow, you unlock its full potential as a content creation powerhouse. The following chapters will delve deeper into the core functionalities of Gemini AI, equipping you to generate top-notch content across various formats and for diverse purposes.

Chapter 3

Demystifying Core Functions: Unlocking the Power of Gemini AI

Congratulations! You've mastered the basics of setting up and navigating Gemini AI. Now, buckle up as we delve into the heart of the matter – exploring its core functionalities and unlocking its true potential for generating high-quality content.

This chapter will equip you with the knowledge and skills to leverage Gemini AI for various content creation needs. Here's a breakdown of the key areas we'll explore:

3.1 Content Generation: From Brainstorming to Full Drafts

Conquering the blank page is a universal struggle for content creators. Gemini AI is here to be your hero, transforming that initial white void into a wellspring of creative content. This section will equip you with the knowledge to leverage Gemini AI for content generation, taking you from brainstorming to full drafts in a streamlined process.

Banishing the Blank Page Blues:

Spark the Flame: Brainstorming with AI: Struggling to come up with content ideas? Gemini AI can be your brainstorming partner. Provide a few broad keywords or a general theme, and let the AI generate a list of potential titles, subheadings, or even outlines to jumpstart your creative process.

Keyword Magic: Keywords are the building blocks of discoverable content. Learn how to incorporate relevant keywords into your prompts to ensure your generated content ranks well in search engine results and reaches your target audience.

Content from a Sample: Have a existing piece of content that needs a refresh? Provide a sample paragraph or snippet to Gemini AI, and explore its ability to expand on the existing content, generate new ideas, or create variations that maintain the core message.

Building Your Content: From Seed to Structured Draft

Content in Chunks: Tailoring Length and Detail: Not all content needs to be a full-length novel. Gemini AI offers flexibility in content length. Specify your needs – a short social media caption, a paragraph for a product description, or a comprehensive blog post outline.

The Power of Prompts: Specificity is Key: Imagine you're giving instructions to a skilled assistant. The clearer your instructions, the better the results. Learn how to craft effective prompts for Gemini AI. This includes specifying the content type (blog post, article, social media caption), target audience (beginners, experts), and the desired tone of voice (formal, casual, humorous).

Structuring Your Content: A well-structured draft forms the foundation of great content. Explore how Gemini AI can assist with creating outlines, incorporating headings and subheadings, and ensuring a logical flow of information throughout your content.

Content Generation on Autopilot: Taking Advantage of AI Creativity

Beyond the Obvious: While providing specific prompts is effective, don't be afraid to experiment with open-ended prompts. See what creative ideas Gemini AI sparks when you give it a starting sentence or a loose thematic direction. You might be surprised by the unique and engaging content it generates.

Building Upon Ideas: The Iterative Approach Don't settle for the first draft. Leverage AI's ability to iterate. Take the initial content generated by Gemini AI, refine it, and provide new prompts based on the draft. This back-and-forth approach can lead to exceptional content that surpasses what you could achieve on your own.

By mastering these techniques, you'll transform Gemini AI into a powerful tool for content generation. The next section explores how to take your content to the next level with the help of AI-powered editing and rewriting functionalities.

3.2 Editing and Rewriting: Refining Your Content with AI Assistance

While AI excels at generating content at scale, the magic touch of human editing remains paramount. This section explores how Gemini AI empowers you to refine and polish your content, ensuring it shines with clarity, accuracy, and impact.

Human + AI: A Collaborative Editing Workflow

Grammar Gremlins and Clarity Chaos: Typos, awkward phrasing, and unclear sentence structure can hinder your content's effectiveness. Let Gemini AI be your grammar checker on steroids. Utilize its built-in editing features to identify and rectify these issues, ensuring your content is polished and professional.

Fact-Checking: The Editor's Responsibility: AI-generated content can be a fantastic starting point, but factual accuracy is your domain. Develop a system for verifying all facts, figures, and statistics presented in your content, especially when leveraging AI-generated text.

AI-powered Rewriting: A Refining Partner: Stuck on a sentence or paragraph that just isn't clicking? Don't despair! Gemini AI can be your rewriting partner. Explore the "rewrite" function to see alternative phrasings and improve the overall flow and readability of your content.

Beyond Grammar and Clarity: Elevating Your Content

Conciseness is King (or Queen): In today's fast-paced world, attention spans are limited. Gemini AI can assist you in identifying areas where your content can be tightened and streamlined. Explore features that suggest ways to condense overly verbose passages and ensure your message is delivered with maximum impact in minimal words.

Engagement Optimization: Captivating your audience is crucial. Learn how to utilize Gemini AI to analyze your content for engagement potential. It might suggest ways to incorporate humor, storytelling elements, or specific vocabulary choices that resonate with your target audience.

SEO Optimization (if applicable): Search engine optimization (SEO) is essential for ensuring your content is discoverable online. Some versions of Gemini AI might offer functionalities to help optimize your content for search engines by suggesting relevant keywords and ensuring proper formatting for search visibility.

Maintaining Your Brand Voice and Style

The Power of Personalization: Gemini AI is a chameleon, able to adapt its writing style to your preferences. Define your brand voice – is it formal and authoritative, casual and conversational, or something in between? Provide clear instructions and examples to train Gemini AI to generate content that reflects your unique brand identity.

Consistency is Key: A strong brand voice relies on consistency. If you have existing style guides or brand voice documentation, consider incorporating them into your workflow. Refer to these resources while working with Gemini AI to ensure all your content adheres to your established brand voice.

Remember: The editing and rewriting functionalities within Gemini AI are there to empower you, not replace your editorial judgment. Use them as valuable tools to streamline your workflow and elevate the quality of your content.

The next section delves into the exciting world of content diversity. We'll explore how Gemini AI can craft content across various formats, catering to your specific needs and target audience.

3.3 Mastering Different Content Formats: Blog Posts, Articles, and More

The beauty of Gemini AI lies in its versatility. It's not a one-trick pony; it can adapt and generate content across a wide range of formats. This section equips you to leverage this strength and create high-quality content tailored to your specific needs.

Content Creation à la Carte: Exploring Different Formats

Blog Posts that Captivate: Blog posts are the cornerstones of many content marketing strategies. Learn how to leverage Gemini AI to craft engaging and informative blog posts. Explore features that assist with:

Generating catchy headlines and introductions.

Structuring your content with clear headings and subheadings.

Creating compelling conclusions with calls to action that drive engagement.

Articles with Impact: Need to establish yourself as a thought leader in your industry? Discover how Gemini AI can be your partner in crafting informative or persuasive articles. Learn how to provide prompts that specify:

The target audience (beginners, experts, or a specific niche).

The desired level of formality (academic journal, online publication, etc.).

The key points you want the article to address.

Beyond the Basics: Expanding Your Content Portfolio

The world of content creation extends far beyond traditional blog posts and articles. Unlock the full potential of Gemini AI by exploring its capabilities for generating content in various formats:

Social Media Magic: Crafting engaging social media captions can be time-consuming. Gemini AI can help! Learn how to generate creative and attention-grabbing captions for different platforms like Twitter, Facebook, or Instagram.

Product Descriptions that Sell: High-converting product descriptions are essential for e-commerce success. Discover how Gemini AI can assist with creating clear, concise, and informative product descriptions that highlight features and benefits, while captivating potential buyers.

Marketing Copy that Converts: Need compelling marketing copy for your website or advertisements? Explore how Gemini AI can generate persuasive and action-oriented copy that resonates with your target audience.

Unleashing Creativity: More Than Just Text

While Gemini AI excels at text generation, it can also spark your creative fire in unexpected ways:

Writing Prompts that Inspire: Struggling to overcome writer's block? Let Gemini AI be your muse! Explore features that generate creative writing prompts across various genres, helping you brainstorm new story ideas and jumpstart your creative process.

Scriptwriting and Story Outlines: For those venturing into the world of video content, Gemini AI might offer functionalities to generate basic story outlines or even script formats, providing a solid foundation for your creative storytelling endeavors.

Remember: As Gemini AI continues to evolve, the range of supported content formats might expand. Stay curious, explore the available features, and experiment to discover how this versatile tool can elevate your content creation across various mediums.

By mastering the content formats explored in this section, you'll be well-equipped to leverage Gemini AI to its full potential. The following chapters will delve deeper into advanced strategies and explore how to integrate Gemini AI seamlessly into your workflow for maximum impact.

Chapter 4

Content Creation on Autopilot: Leveraging Gemini AI's Advanced Features

Congratulations! You've mastered the fundamentals of navigating Gemini AI and generating high-quality content across various formats. Now, buckle up as we explore the exciting world of advanced features, designed to transform you from a content creator into a content creation machine! This chapter equips you with the knowledge to unlock the full potential of Gemini AI and automate repetitive tasks, allowing you to focus on strategic initiatives.

4.1 Utilizing Templates and Workflows: Streamlining Your Content Creation Process

Content creation can feel like an endless cycle of starting from scratch. Imagine a world where you can automate repetitive tasks and have a blueprint readily available for your most common content formats. This is the magic of templates and workflows within Gemini AI! By leveraging these features, you can transform your workflow from reactive to proactive, freeing up time and mental energy for strategic thinking.

Template Magic: Pre-Defined Content Blueprints

Building Your Content Arsenal: Templates act as pre-defined structures for your content, serving as a launchpad for consistent and efficient content creation. Explore how to create templates within Gemini AI. These templates can include:

Intros and Outros: Craft compelling opening paragraphs and strong conclusions that can be easily adapted to different content pieces.

Formatting Elements: Include elements like bulleted lists, headers, and subheadings within your templates to ensure consistent formatting across your content.

Brand Specific Elements: Incorporate your brand voice, tone, and even specific keywords or phrases directly into your templates to streamline content creation and maintain brand consistency.

Template Application in Action: Let's say you create a blog post template that includes an intro, two subheading sections, a bulleted list section, and a call-to-action outro. Whenever you need to write a new blog post, you can simply select this template and fill in the blanks with your specific content. This saves you time from formatting and structuring your content from scratch, allowing you to focus on the core message you want to convey.

Workflows: The Art of Automation

Building Your Content Creation Conveyor Belt: Imagine a step-by-step process tailored to your specific content creation needs. Workflows allow you to automate repetitive tasks within Gemini AI, creating a smooth and efficient production line for your content.

Designing Your Workflow: When creating a workflow, you can specify actions and prompts for Gemini AI to follow at each stage. Here's a breakdown of the process:

Define the workflow steps: Will it involve generating an initial draft, suggesting headlines, and then checking for readability?

Set prompts for each step: Provide clear instructions for Gemini AI at each stage of the workflow.

Integrate templates: Incorporate your pre-defined templates into your workflows to ensure consistent formatting and branding.

Workflow in Action: Let's say you design a workflow for creating social media captions. Your workflow might involve prompting Gemini AI to generate a few different captions based on a specific blog post, then allowing you to choose the best one and automatically resizing it to fit the character limits of different social media platforms.

The Power of Combining Templates and Workflows

The true magic happens when you combine templates and workflows. Imagine having a social media content workflow that automatically generates captions based on your blog post template, ensuring consistent messaging across platforms.

By leveraging templates and workflows, you can significantly reduce the time and effort required for content creation. This allows you to focus on the strategic aspects, like brainstorming new content ideas, tailoring content to specific audience segments, and measuring the performance of your content marketing efforts.

The next section explores project management and collaboration functionalities within Gemini AI, empowering you to streamline your workflow even further and seamlessly integrate content creation with your team.

4.2 Exploring Content Styles and Tones: Finding the Perfect Voice for Your Audience

In the world of content creation, one size does not fit all. Just like fashion, your content needs to reflect a style and tone that resonates with your target audience. This chapter delves into the exciting world of content styles and tones within Gemini AI, equipping you with the knowledge to craft content that speaks directly to your readers and ignites engagement.

4.2.1 Understanding Content Style: The Look and Feel of Your Content

Beyond Just Words: Content style goes beyond the technical aspects of grammar and syntax. It's the overall presentation and character of your content. Consider the following elements that contribute to content style:

Sentence Structure: Are your sentences short and punchy, or long and descriptive?

Word Choice: Do you use formal vocabulary or a more casual, conversational tone?

Figurative Language: Do you incorporate metaphors, similes, or other figures of speech to add flair and depth?

4.2.2 A Spectrum of Styles: Tailoring Your Content to Specific Needs

Informative Style: Think academic journals or news articles. This style prioritizes clarity, accuracy, and objectivity.

Persuasive Style: The goal here is to convince the reader to take a specific action. This style often uses strong verbs, emotional appeals, and logical reasoning.

Narrative Style: Storytelling is a powerful tool for engagement. This style focuses on characters, plot, and creating an emotional connection with the reader.

Conversational Style: Imagine having a chat with a friend. This style is informal, friendly, and uses a more relaxed tone.

4.2.3 Striking the Right Tone: Aligning with Your Audience

Understanding Your Audience: The key to effective content lies in understanding who you're writing for. Consider your target audience's demographics, interests, and level of expertise on the topic.

Aligning Tone with Audience: Once you understand your audience, you can choose the tone that best resonates with them. Here are some examples:

Formal tone for professional audiences or complex topics.

Informal tone for younger demographics or social media content.

Humorous tone for a lighthearted and engaging approach.

Authoritative tone to establish yourself as an expert.

4.2.4 Using Gemini AI to Achieve Your Desired Style and Tone

Gemini AI is your chameleon content creation partner! Here's how to leverage it to achieve your desired style and tone:

Provide Clear Instructions: When crafting prompts for Gemini AI, specify the style you're aiming for. Include keywords like "informative," "persuasive," "conversational," or "humorous" to guide the AI in the right direction.

Refine and Iterate: The first draft might not always perfectly capture the desired tone. Utilize Gemini AI's rewriting functionalities to experiment with different phrasings and ensure your content achieves the perfect balance of style and tone for your audience.

Remember: While Gemini AI provides powerful tools, your editorial judgment remains crucial. Refine the generated content to ensure it aligns with your brand voice and resonates with your target audience.

By mastering the art of content style and tone, you can transform your content from informative text to a captivating force that engages your audience and drives results. The next section explores advanced prompt engineering techniques, empowering you to provide even more specific instructions to Gemini AI and unlock its full potential for content creation.

4.3 Integrating with Other Tools: Supercharge Your Workflow with Seamless Integrations

Imagine a world where your content creation process flows effortlessly, with Gemini AI seamlessly interacting with the tools you already use. This is the magic of integration! This section explores how to connect Gemini AI with other applications, empowering you to streamline your workflow and maximize efficiency.

4.3.1 Building Your Content Creation Ecosystem

Beyond a Standalone Tool: While Gemini AI is a powerful content creation tool, its true potential is unleashed when integrated with the arsenal of applications you already rely on. Here are some potential integrations to consider:

Grammar Checkers and Plagiarism Detection Tools: Ensure your content is polished and error-free by integrating with grammar checkers like Grammarly or plagiarism checkers like Copyscape.

Content Management Systems (CMS): Streamline your publishing process by integrating with your CMS (e.g., WordPress, HubSpot). This allows you to seamlessly transfer generated content directly into your CMS for easy publishing.

Marketing Automation Platforms: For those using marketing automation platforms like Mailchimp or Constant Contact, explore integration options to leverage Gemini AI for crafting compelling email marketing content or social media posts.

4.3.2 The Benefits of Integration

Reduced Manual Work: Integrations eliminate the need for manual data transfer and repetitive tasks. Imagine crafting social media captions in Gemini AI and automatically having them sized correctly for different platforms.

Improved Accuracy and Consistency: Integrations with grammar checkers and plagiarism checkers ensure your content is polished and error-free, maintaining a high standard of quality.

Enhanced Efficiency: By streamlining your workflow through integrations, you can free up valuable time and focus on strategic content marketing initiatives.

4.3.3 Exploring Integration Options (if applicable)

The specific integration options available within Gemini AI might depend on the version you're using and the external tools you leverage. Here's a general roadmap for exploring integration possibilities:

Reviewing Gemini AI Documentation: Start by consulting the official Gemini AI documentation or help section. Look for information on supported integrations or an API (Application Programming Interface) that allows for custom integrations with other tools.

Third-Party App Marketplaces: Many content creation and marketing tools offer app marketplaces where you can browse and connect with various integrations. Search for integrations between Gemini AI and your specific tools of choice.

The Future of Integration: Streamlined Workflows and Automation

As technology evolves, expect even more seamless integrations between Gemini AI and other creative tools. Imagine a future where content flows effortlessly from ideation in brainstorming apps to generation in Gemini AI, and finally to publication through your CMS or marketing automation platform.

By leveraging integrations, you can transform your workflow from disjointed tasks to a well-oiled content creation machine. This allows you to focus on the strategic aspects of content marketing and achieve exceptional results. The following chapter dives into the world of content analytics and optimization, empowering you to measure the success of your content and refine your approach for maximum impact.

Chapter 5

Cracking the Code: Content Strategies for Maximum Impact with Gemini AI

Congratulations! You've unlocked the advanced functionalities of Gemini AI and are well on your way to becoming a content creation powerhouse. But content creation is not just about churning out text. It's about crafting strategic pieces that resonate with your audience, achieve your marketing goals, and deliver measurable results. This chapter equips you with the knowledge to develop effective content strategies and leverage Gemini AI to fuel your content marketing success.

5.1 Defining Your Content Goals: Aligning Gemini AI with Your Content Strategy

Content creation, like any endeavor, thrives with a clear direction. Before diving headfirst into crafting content with Gemini AI, it's important to establish your content marketing goals. By understanding what you want to achieve, you can leverage Gemini AI's functionalities to develop a targeted content strategy that delivers measurable results.

Why Content Marketing Matters: Setting the Stage for Success

Think of content marketing as a strategic conversation with your target audience. It's about creating informative, engaging, and valuable content that attracts potential customers, fosters brand loyalty, and ultimately drives business growth. Here are some of the key benefits of a well-defined content marketing strategy:

Increased Brand Awareness: High-quality content positions you as a thought leader in your industry, making your brand more recognizable and trustworthy.

Lead Generation: Effective content attracts potential customers who are interested in the problems you solve. By providing valuable resources and establishing your expertise, you can capture leads and nurture them into paying customers.

Boosted Website Traffic: Compelling content naturally draws visitors to your website or blog. This increases brand exposure and creates opportunities to convert visitors into leads or customers.

Enhanced Customer Engagement: Content marketing fosters a two-way conversation with your audience. By providing valuable content and addressing their needs, you build stronger relationships with your customer base.

Setting SMART Content Marketing Goals

Now that you understand the "why" behind content marketing, let's move on to the "how." The key to success lies in setting **SMART** goals for your content marketing efforts. SMART stands for:

Specific: Clearly define what you want to achieve. Don't just say "increase brand awareness." Instead, aim for "increase brand awareness by 20% within the next quarter."

Measurable: Establish metrics to track your progress. This could involve website traffic, lead generation, social media engagement, or conversion rates.

Attainable: Set goals that are ambitious yet achievable. Consider your resources and target audience when setting realistic goals.

Relevant: Ensure your goals align with your overall marketing objectives and business strategy.

Time-Bound: Set a timeframe for achieving your goals. This creates a sense of urgency and keeps you accountable.

Examples of SMART Content Marketing Goals:

Generate 100 qualified leads through blog content within the next 3 months.

Increase website traffic by 15% over the next quarter through SEO-optimized content creation.

Improve brand awareness by achieving 500 mentions on social media platforms within the next 6 months.

By setting SMART goals, you provide a clear roadmap for your content marketing strategy. The following section explores how to translate these goals into actionable steps using Gemini AI.

5.2 Building a Content Calendar with AI: Planning and Scheduling Made Easy

Now that you've established your SMART content marketing goals (cue high fives!), it's time to translate them into a tangible action plan. This is where a content calendar comes into play. Think of it as your roadmap to content creation success, ensuring a consistent flow of content that aligns with your goals and target audience. Here's how Gemini AI can be your secret weapon for building a powerful content calendar:

From Goals to Themes: Charting Your Content Course

Content Pillars and Topic Clusters: Imagine an organized filing cabinet for your content. Content pillars are the broad topics that resonate with your audience and your industry. For example, if you're a bakery, your content pillars might be "baking tips," "cake decorating ideas," or "healthy dessert recipes." Topic clusters are more specific subtopics that branch out from these pillars. For instance, under the "baking tips" pillar, you might have topic clusters on "bread baking basics," "perfecting pie crusts," or "substitutes for common baking ingredients." By using Gemini AI, you can brainstorm pillar ideas and delve deeper to generate engaging subtopics that cater to your audience's search intent.

Brainstorming Bonanza: Generating Content Ideas with Gemini AI

Overcoming the Blank Page Blues: Staring at a blank cursor can be daunting. Gemini AI can jumpstart your creative process by providing a treasure trove of content ideas. Here's how to leverage its functionalities:

Keyword Exploration: Provide Gemini AI with relevant keywords related to your chosen content pillars. The AI can then generate a list of potential subtopics, headlines, and even blog post outlines, giving you a springboard for creating informative and engaging content.

Content Format Inspiration: Not sure what format would resonate best with your audience for a specific topic? Gemini AI can help! Provide a brief description of your topic and let the AI suggest different content formats, such as blog posts, articles, infographics, or even video scripts.

Building Your Content Calendar: Scheduling Success

Mapping Goals to Content: Once you have a list of potential content ideas, use your SMART goals as a filter. Prioritize topics that directly address your goals and resonate with your target audience.

Scheduling for Success: With your prioritized content ideas in hand, it's time to schedule them in your calendar. Gemini AI might integrate with popular calendar applications, allowing you to seamlessly schedule content creation tasks and publishing dates within your existing workflow.

Maintaining Consistency: The key to content marketing success is consistency. Use your calendar to plan content in advance, ensuring a steady stream of fresh content to keep your audience engaged.

Remember: Your content calendar is a living document. As you gather data and track your progress, you can refine your calendar and adapt your content strategy for even better results.

The following section explores different content types you can create with Gemini AI, catering to various audience needs and marketing objectives.

5.3 Optimizing Content for Search Engines: Leveraging AI for SEO Success

In today's digital landscape, ranking high on search engine results pages (SERPs) is paramount to driving organic traffic and achieving your content marketing goals. This is where Search Engine Optimization (SEO) comes into play. By incorporating SEO best practices, you ensure your content is discoverable by your target audience when they search for relevant keywords. Here's how Gemini AI can be your SEO superpower, optimizing your content for maximum visibility.

Understanding Search Intent: Decoding What Users Are Looking For

The Power of Keywords: Keywords are the foundation of SEO. They represent the terms or phrases users enter into search engines. By understanding the search intent behind relevant keywords, you can tailor your content to provide the information users are actively seeking. Gemini AI can assist you with keyword research, suggesting terms with high search volume and low competition, allowing you to target the right audience while avoiding oversaturated keywords.

On-Page Optimization: Optimizing Your Content for Search Engines

Title Tags and Meta Descriptions: These are like billboards for your content, displayed on SERPs. Gemini AI can help you craft compelling title tags and meta descriptions that are not only informative but also optimized with relevant keywords to entice users to click on your content.

Content Structure and Formatting: Search engines favor well-structured content that is easy for users to navigate and understand. Gemini AI can help you format your content with clear headings, subheadings, and bullet points, making it scannable and improving readability for both users and search engine crawlers.

Internal Linking: Linking to relevant content within your website keeps users engaged and helps search engines understand the structure and hierarchy of your website. Gemini AI can analyze your existing content and suggest relevant internal linking opportunities to improve website navigation and user experience.

AI-Powered Content Optimization: Taking SEO to the Next Level

Staying Ahead of the Curve: SEO algorithms are constantly evolving. Gemini AI can stay abreast of the latest SEO trends and best practices. By leveraging its functionalities, you can ensure your content is optimized according to the latest ranking factors, giving you a competitive edge in search results.

Content Quality and Relevancy: Search engines prioritize high-quality content that is relevant to user search intent. Gemini AI can analyze your content for readability, clarity, and topical relevance, ensuring it meets the standards that search engines value.

Data-Driven Insights: Don't just guess what works – use data to guide your SEO strategy. Gemini AI might offer features that analyze your content's SEO performance. Use these insights to identify areas for improvement and refine your content for even better organic reach.

The Future of SEO: AI-Powered Personalization and Topic Authority

As AI technology continues to develop, the future of SEO is brimming with exciting possibilities:

Personalized Search Results: Imagine search engines that consider a user's individual search history and preferences to deliver hyper-personalized results. Content optimized for user intent and searcher behavior will likely hold even greater SEO value.

Topic Authority and Expertise: AI might play a role in determining a website's topical authority and expertise on a particular subject. Creating high-quality, informative content that establishes your brand as a thought leader in your niche will be crucial for achieving long-term SEO success.

By leveraging Gemini AI for SEO optimization, you can ensure your content is discoverable, informative, and valuable to your target audience. This will not only drive organic traffic but also establish your brand as a leader in your industry. The following section delves into the world of content promotion and distribution, empowering you to get your content in front of the right eyes.

Chapter 6

Beyond the Basics: Advanced Techniques for Mastering Gemini AI

Congratulations! You've unlocked the core functionalities of Gemini AI and are well on your way to becoming a content creation pro. This chapter ventures into the exciting world of advanced techniques, empowering you to push the boundaries of what's possible and truly master Gemini AI.

6.1 Fine-Tuning Your Prompts: Crafting Instructions that Generate Stellar Content:

The Power of the Prompt: Your Roadmap to Success

The prompt you provide to Gemini AI acts as the foundation for the content it generates. Just like a detailed map guides you to your destination, a clear and concise prompt steers the AI in the right direction, ensuring the generated content aligns with your vision.

Essential Elements of a Powerful Prompt:

Target Audience: Who are you creating this content for? Understanding your target audience's demographics, interests, and level of expertise allows you to tailor the content for better comprehension and engagement.

Example: "Target audience: Marketing professionals with experience in social media marketing."

Content Goal: What do you want to achieve with this content? Do you want to inform, persuade, entertain, or evoke a specific emotion?

Example: "Content Goal: Inform the audience about the latest social media marketing trends."

Desired Style and Tone: How do you want the content to sound? Formal, informal, conversational, serious, humorous? Providing specific instructions on style and tone ensures the AI generates content that matches your brand voice and resonates with your audience.

Example: "Desired Style and Tone: Informative and concise, using a professional tone."

Keywords and References: Provide relevant keywords and phrases to guide the AI's content direction. Including links or snippets of existing content as reference points can further illustrate the desired style, tone, and content direction.

Example: "Keywords: social media marketing trends, 2024, audience engagement. References: [Link to a recent article on social media marketing trends]."

Refining Your Prompts: An Iterative Process

The first draft generated by Gemini AI might not always be perfect. This is where the iterative process of prompt refinement comes into play. Here's how to achieve optimal results:

Review the Generated Content: Carefully analyze the AI-generated content to see how well it aligns with your initial prompt.

Identify Areas for Improvement: Are there any sections that lack clarity, miss the target tone, or stray from the intended message?

Refine Your Prompt: Based on your analysis, revise your prompt to provide more specific instructions or adjust the keywords and references to guide the AI in the right direction.

Regenerate and Revise: Once you've refined your prompt, regenerate the content and repeat the review process until you achieve the desired outcome.

Remember: Don't be afraid to experiment with different prompts and phrasing. The more specific and detailed you are, the better Gemini AI will understand your requirements and generate content that exceeds your expectations.

By following these guidelines and embracing an iterative approach, you can master the art of crafting prompts that unlock the full potential of Gemini AI and generate stellar content that achieves your goals.

6.2 Overcoming Creative Blocks: Using AI to Spark New Ideas and Inspiration

We've all been there: staring at a blank cursor, mind devoid of ideas. Creative block can be a real struggle for any content creator. But fear not! Gemini AI can be your secret weapon to overcome creative roadblocks and reignite your imaginative spark.

Understanding Creative Block: The Culprit Behind the Blank Page

Creative block can stem from various factors, including stress, burnout, or simply feeling uninspired. It can be a frustrating experience, hindering your content creation workflow.

How Gemini AI Can Help You Blast Through Creative Block

Here's how Gemini AI can be your creative muse, helping you generate new ideas and overcome creative block:

Brainstorming Bonanza:

Keyword Exploration: Provide Gemini AI with broad keywords related to your topic or niche. The AI can then generate a list of subtopics, headlines, and even blog post outlines, giving you a springboard for fresh ideas.

Content Format Inspiration: Stuck in a rut with repetitive content formats? Give Gemini AI a try! Provide a brief description of your topic and let the AI suggest different formats to explore, like blog posts, articles, infographics, or even video scripts. This can nudge you outside your comfort zone and spark new creative approaches.

Overcoming the Blank Page Blues:

Seed Content Creation: Don't have a starting point? Provide Gemini AI with a single sentence or a short paragraph related to your topic. The AI can then build upon that seed content, expanding it into a more substantial piece, giving you a foundation to develop further.

Unexpected Twists and Turns: Let's say you're writing a blog post about social media marketing trends. Feeling uninspired by the usual suspects? Instruct Gemini AI to generate content about social media marketing trends, but with a focus on a specific industry you might not have considered before. This approach can lead to unexpected and interesting content angles.

Reframe Your Perspective:

Different Content Perspectives: Sometimes a shift in perspective can breathe new life into your content. Instruct Gemini AI to rewrite a section of your existing content from a different angle, such as a customer testimonial or an expert interview format. This can help you see your topic from a fresh viewpoint and uncover new ideas.

Remember: AI is a powerful tool, but it doesn't replace human creativity. Use Gemini AI's suggestions as a springboard to ignite your own creative spark. Refine and build upon the AI-generated ideas to craft unique and engaging content that resonates with your audience.

Beyond Overcoming Block: Exploring New Creative Horizons

Gemini AI can also be a valuable tool for exploring new creative territories you might not have ventured into before. For instance, you could use it to:

Develop Story Concepts: If you're working on a creative writing project, use Gemini AI to brainstorm story ideas, character profiles, or plot outlines.

Craft Compelling Ad Copy: Stuck on crafting captivating ad copy? Provide Gemini AI with your product or service description and target audience details, and let the AI generate creative and persuasive copy that grabs attention.

By embracing experimentation and using Gemini AI as a creative partner, you can overcome creative block, unlock new ideas, and produce captivating content that stands out from the crowd.

6.3 Fact-Checking and Verification: Maintaining Accuracy in AI-Generated Content

While Gemini AI is a powerful tool for content creation, it's important to remember that it leverages machine learning models trained on massive datasets of text and code. This means the generated content, while informative and creative, might require verification to ensure accuracy, especially for factual topics.

Why Fact-Checking is Crucial:

Maintaining credibility and trust with your audience is paramount. Inaccurate information can damage your reputation and compromise the effectiveness of your content marketing efforts.

Developing a Robust Fact-Checking Process:

Here's how to establish a system for ensuring the accuracy of AI-generated content:

Credibility of Sources: When Gemini AI incorporates information from external sources during content generation, it might provide citations or links. Always critically evaluate these sources to ensure their credibility and trustworthiness. Reputable sources include academic journals, government websites, and established news organizations.

Double-Checking Facts: Don't rely solely on AI-generated content, particularly for statistical data, historical information, or scientific claims. Conduct your own fact-checking using trustworthy sources to verify the accuracy of the information presented.

Cross-Referencing with Multiple Sources: Never rely on a single source for verification. Consult multiple credible sources to confirm the accuracy of facts and statistics mentioned in the AI-generated content.

Leveraging Gemini AI for Enhanced Fact-Checking:

While the onus of fact-checking lies with you, Gemini AI can still be a valuable tool in this process:

Identifying Potential Issues: Gemini AI might highlight sections of the generated content that require further verification. Look for phrases like "according to a study" or "estimates suggest" as indicators that additional fact-checking might be necessary.

Fact-Checking Automation Tools: Explore integration options with fact-checking automation tools that can analyze the AI-generated content and identify inconsistencies or potentially inaccurate information. These tools can be a time-saving measure, but it's still crucial to exercise your own judgment and verify the flagged information.

Remember: Fact-checking is an ongoing process. As new information comes to light, revisit your content periodically to ensure it remains accurate and up-to-date.

Maintaining Transparency: Disclosing the Use of AI

While the use of AI for content creation is becoming increasingly common, transparency is key. Consider including a disclosure within your content mentioning that AI was used in the content generation process. This fosters trust with your audience and demonstrates your commitment to providing accurate and verified information.

By establishing a robust fact-checking process and leveraging the functionalities of Gemini AI, you can ensure your content is not only informative and engaging but also factually accurate and trustworthy. This will solidify your brand reputation and allow you to achieve your content marketing goals with confidence.

Chapter 7

The Art of Human-AI Collaboration: Working Effectively with Gemini AI

Congratulations! You've delved into the depths of Gemini AI, explored its functionalities, and unlocked its potential for generating creative and informative content. This chapter dives into the heart of human-AI collaboration, empowering you to work effectively with Gemini AI to achieve exceptional content creation results.

7.1 Understanding the Role of AI: A Tool to Empower, Not Replace

The world of content creation is undergoing a significant transformation. Artificial intelligence (AI) tools like Gemini AI are making waves, but it's important to understand that AI is here to **collaborate** and **empower**, not replace human creators.

AI: A Powerful Assistant, Not a Replacement

Fears about AI replacing human content creators are understandable. However, AI's true strength lies in its ability to **augment** human capabilities. Here's why:

Content Generation at Scale: AI can churn out vast amounts of content in various formats, freeing up your time for strategic tasks like concept development and audience analysis.

Enhanced Creativity: AI can spark new ideas and overcome creative block by generating unexpected content formats or exploring different angles on a topic.

Data-Driven Insights: AI can analyze data to identify audience preferences and content performance metrics, allowing you to tailor your content for maximum impact.

The Irreplaceable Human Touch

While AI excels at content generation and data processing, human creators bring irreplaceable qualities to the table:

Strategic Storytelling: You define the narrative, set the goals, and determine the target audience. Your vision guides the AI in creating content that aligns with your brand message and resonates with your readers.

Critical Thinking and Analysis: AI-generated content might require verification and editing to ensure accuracy, factuality, and adherence to brand voice and editorial standards. Your critical thinking skills are crucial for polishing the final product.

Emotional Intelligence and Audience Understanding: You possess an innate understanding of human emotions and audience behavior. This allows you to craft content that evokes the desired response, builds connections, and fosters brand loyalty.

The Future of Content Creation: A Human-AI Symphony

The future of content creation belongs to the powerful synergy between humans and AI. Imagine a world where:

AI handles the heavy lifting: Content generation, data analysis, and research become streamlined processes managed by AI.

Humans focus on high-value tasks: You dedicate your time and expertise to strategic planning, audience engagement, and content promotion.

AI and humans collaborate creatively: Brainstorming sessions are enhanced by AI suggesting unique ideas and providing data-driven insights to fuel creative exploration.

The Takeaway: A New Era of Storytelling

The human-AI partnership signifies a new chapter in content creation. By embracing AI as a powerful tool, you can unlock a world of creative possibilities, craft content that resonates with your audience on a deeper level, and achieve remarkable results in your content marketing endeavors. The future is not about AI replacing human storytellers, but rather about humans and AI working together to create a more impactful and engaging storytelling experience.

7.2 Maintaining Editorial Control: Ensuring Your Brand Voice and Quality

Even with the impressive capabilities of AI-powered content creation tools like Gemini AI, maintaining editorial control is paramount. This ensures your content adheres to your brand voice, quality standards, and messaging, ultimately safeguarding your brand identity and reputation.

The Importance of Editorial Control

Here's why editorial control is crucial in the age of AI content creation:

Brand Consistency: Your brand voice is your unique personality. It's how you communicate with your audience and establish trust. Editorial control ensures that AI-generated content aligns with your brand voice, maintaining consistency across all your content pieces.

Quality Assurance: While AI can generate impressive content, it may not always be perfect. Editorial control allows you to identify and address any factual inaccuracies, grammatical errors, or inconsistencies in tone or style.

Meeting Audience Expectations: Your audience expects a certain level of quality and value from your content. Editorial control guarantees that the AI-generated content meets those expectations by ensuring it's informative, engaging, and tailored to your target audience's needs.

Strategies for Effective Editorial Control with AI

Here's how to leverage Gemini AI while maintaining editorial control over your content:

Clearly Defined Brand Guidelines: Develop clear brand guidelines that outline your brand voice, tone, messaging, and editorial style. These guidelines serve as a reference point for both you and the AI when generating content.

Crafting Compelling Prompts: The quality of your prompts significantly impacts the output generated by AI. Provide clear instructions that specify the target audience, content goals, desired style, and tone. Include relevant keywords and reference examples to guide the AI in the right direction.

Review and Refine Iteratively: The first draft is rarely the final product. Develop a review process where you meticulously analyze the AI-generated content, identify areas for improvement, and refine your prompts to achieve the desired outcome.

Fact-Checking and Verification: Don't rely solely on AI for factual accuracy. Double-check all statistics, claims, and data with credible sources, especially for sensitive topics.

Human Editing Expertise: AI-generated content often benefits from a human touch. Editors can ensure proper grammar, sentence structure, and overall clarity, while also refining the content to match your brand voice perfectly.

Gemini AI: Empowering You to Maintain Control

Here's how Gemini AI can facilitate editorial control:

Content Templates: Create templates within Gemini AI that incorporate your brand voice, tone, and stylistic elements. This ensures consistency across your content even when leveraging AI for generation.

Style Guides Integration: Explore integration options with style guides or brand voice dictionaries. This allows Gemini AI to reference these resources while generating content, further ensuring adherence to your editorial standards.

Content Quality Analysis Features: Some features within Gemini AI might analyze readability, clarity, and SEO optimization of your content. Utilize these features to identify areas for improvement and maintain high-quality content.

The Future of Editorial Control with AI

As AI technology advances, the future of editorial control promises exciting possibilities:

AI-Powered Brand Voice Analysis: Imagine AI that analyzes your existing content and marketing materials to identify and replicate your brand voice with even greater precision.

Real-Time Feedback and Optimization: AI might provide real-time feedback on the brand alignment and quality of the generated content, allowing for on-the-fly adjustments and refinements.

Smarter Content Insights: AI could analyze content performance data to identify what resonates best with your audience, informing future content creation strategies and editorial decisions.

The Final Word: A Collaborative Effort

Maintaining editorial control with AI is not about micromanaging the process. It's about fostering a collaborative effort. You provide the vision and strategic direction, while AI augments your capabilities with its content generation and analysis skills. By working together, you can achieve exceptional results while safeguarding your brand identity and delivering high-quality content that truly connects with your audience.

7.3 The Future of Human-AI Partnerships: Building a Sustainable Workflow

The future of content creation belongs to the harmonious collaboration between humans and AI. By leveraging the strengths of both, you can streamline content creation processes, achieve exceptional results, and stay ahead of the curve in the ever-evolving digital landscape. This section dives into building a sustainable workflow that fosters this powerful human-AI partnership.

Optimizing the Human-AI Workflow for Long-Term Success

Here's how to establish a sustainable workflow that optimizes the human-AI collaboration for content creation:

Clearly Defined Roles and Responsibilities: Clearly outline the roles of human creators and AI within your content creation process. Humans should focus on strategic tasks like content planning, audience analysis, and editorial control. AI excels at content generation, data processing, and repetitive tasks.

Establish Seamless Communication Channels: Ensure clear and efficient communication between human content creators and AI. This might involve using project management tools, content briefs, and feedback mechanisms to ensure everyone stays aligned throughout the workflow.

Embrace Continuous Learning: The world of AI is constantly evolving. Stay up-to-date on the latest advancements in AI content creation tools and best practices. Encourage ongoing exploration and experimentation to maximize the potential of your human-AI partnership.

Prioritize Measurement and Iteration: Track the performance of your AI-generated content. Analyze metrics like engagement, traffic, and conversions to identify what works well and where improvements can be made. Continuously refine your prompts, content strategies, and overall workflow based on data-driven insights.

The Future of AI-Assisted Content Creation

As AI technology matures, the future of human-AI partnerships in content creation promises exciting possibilities:

AI That Adapts to Your Workflow: Imagine AI that seamlessly integrates into your existing content creation workflow, learning your preferences and adapting its functionalities to best support your creative process.

AI-Powered Content Insights and Recommendations: AI might analyze vast amounts of data to provide personalized recommendations on content topics, formats, and styles that are likely to resonate with your target audience.

The Rise of AI as a Creative Brainstorming Partner: The future holds immense potential for AI to evolve beyond content generation and into a true creative brainstorming partner. Imagine brainstorming sessions where AI contributes unique ideas, explores different creative angles, and even helps overcome writer's block.

The Power of Human-AI Synergy

The future of content creation is not a competition between humans and AI, but rather a powerful collaboration. By embracing AI as a tool to empower your creativity and streamline your workflow, you can unlock a new era of content creation possibilities. This human-AI synergy will allow you to produce high-quality content that resonates with your audience, achieves your marketing goals, and positions you for long-term success in the ever-changing digital world.

Chapter 8

Ethical Considerations of AI-Generated Content

The remarkable capabilities of AI-powered content creation tools like Gemini AI come hand-in-hand with important ethical considerations. As you leverage AI to streamline your content creation process, it's crucial to be mindful of the potential impact and ensure your practices are ethical and responsible.

8.1 Transparency and Disclosure: Informing Your Audience about AI Use:

Building Trust Through Transparency

In the realm of AI-generated content, transparency is paramount. Disclosing the use of AI in your content creation process fosters trust and allows your audience to make informed decisions about the information they consume.

Why Transparency Matters

Trustworthy Content, Trustworthy Creator: Transparency builds trust with your audience. By disclosing the use of AI, you demonstrate honesty and integrity, solidifying your reputation as a reliable source of information.

Informed Decisions: When your audience understands how your content is created, they can make informed decisions about how they engage with it. Transparency empowers your readers.

Approaches to Disclosure

Clear and Concise Statements: Consider including a straightforward statement within your content mentioning that AI was used in the content generation process.

Example: "This content was created with the assistance of Gemini AI, a large language model."

Disclosures Within Content or Author Bios: You can incorporate the disclosure within your content itself, like an author's bio, or at the end of the piece.

Finding the Right Balance

While transparency is essential, avoid overly technical explanations that might confuse your audience. Focus on delivering the message clearly and concisely.

Transparency Beyond Disclosure

Transparency extends beyond simply mentioning AI use. Here are some additional considerations:

Differentiating Human and AI Contributions: It's important to distinguish between sections written by humans and those generated by AI. This can be done through subtle cues or annotations.

Providing Context About AI's Role: Briefly explain how AI was used in the content creation process. Did it generate outlines, complete drafts, or provide research assistance?

The Future of Transparency in AI Content Creation

As AI content creation becomes more commonplace, transparency standards might evolve. Here are some potential future scenarios:

Industry Standards and Best Practices: Standardized guidelines or best practices for disclosing AI use in content creation might emerge within specific industries.

Transparency Labels or Badges: Imagine content creators displaying badges or labels on their content to indicate the use of AI.

By prioritizing transparency, you can foster trust with your audience, empower them to make informed decisions, and contribute to a future of responsible AI content creation.

8.2 Combating Bias: Ensuring Fairness and Accuracy in AI-Generated Content

AI-powered content creation tools like Gemini AI are incredibly powerful, but it's vital to address potential biases that can creep into AI-generated content. These biases can stem from the data used to train AI models, and if left unchecked, can lead to inaccurate or unfair content. This section dives into how to mitigate bias and ensure the fairness and accuracy of your AI-generated content.

Understanding the Root of Bias in AI Content

Biased Training Data: AI models are trained on massive datasets of text and code. If this data contains inherent biases, these biases can be reflected in the AI's outputs. For instance, an AI trained on news articles might perpetuate gender stereotypes if those stereotypes are prevalent within the training data.

Algorithmic Bias: The algorithms used to develop AI models can also introduce bias. For example, algorithms might prioritize certain types of data over others, leading to skewed content generation.

The Dangers of Biased Content

Misinformation and Stereotypes: Biased AI content can perpetuate misinformation and stereotypes, hindering social progress and marginalizing certain groups.

Loss of Credibility: If your audience perceives your content as biased, it can damage your credibility and reputation.

Strategies for Mitigating Bias

Diverse Training Data Sets: The foundation of mitigating bias lies in using diverse and inclusive training data sets. This ensures that the AI is exposed to a variety of perspectives and viewpoints, reducing the influence of inherent biases.

Human Oversight and Review: Even with diverse training data, human oversight remains crucial. Review AI-generated content for potential biases and edit or refine the content to ensure fairness and accuracy.

Fairness Tools and Techniques: There are AI fairness tools being developed to help identify and mitigate bias in AI models. Explore these tools to further safeguard against biased content generation.

Combating Bias Throughout the Workflow

Identify Your Biases: The first step is acknowledging that we all have biases. Be mindful of your own biases and how they might influence your prompts and instructions to the AI.

Prompt Engineering: Carefully craft your prompts to guide the AI in the right direction. Use inclusive language and avoid stereotypes in your instructions.

Fact-Checking and Verification: Don't rely solely on AI-generated content, especially for sensitive topics. Fact-check the information to ensure accuracy and verify the absence of bias.

The Future of Fair and Accurate AI Content Creation

Advancements in AI Fairness Research: As AI fairness research progresses, we can expect more sophisticated tools and techniques to emerge for identifying and mitigating bias in AI models.

Standardized Best Practices: The future might hold standardized best practices for developing and using AI content creation tools in a fair and unbiased manner.

Focus on Responsible AI Development: Continued emphasis on responsible AI development is essential to ensure that AI is used ethically and produces unbiased and accurate content.

Conclusion

By acknowledging the potential for bias and implementing these mitigation strategies, you can ensure that your AI-generated content is fair, accurate, and trustworthy. This allows you to leverage the power of AI while promoting responsible and ethical AI practices.

8.3 The Future of AI and Responsible Content Creation

The future of AI and content creation is brimming with exciting possibilities. As AI technology continues to evolve, we can expect advancements in several key areas that will foster even more responsible and impactful content creation:

1. Enhanced Fairness and Mitigating Bias

AI Fairness Tools and Techniques: We can expect significant advancements in AI fairness tools that can automatically detect and mitigate bias in training data sets and algorithms. This will lead to AI-generated content that is more balanced, inclusive, and representative of diverse perspectives.

Standardized Best Practices: The development of standardized best practices for building and using AI content creation tools with fairness in mind will become increasingly important. These guidelines will ensure a more responsible and ethical approach to AI-powered content generation across industries.

2. Transparency and User Control

Transparency Standards and Regulations: Clear industry standards and potential regulations might emerge to govern the use and disclosure of AI-generated content. This will empower users with more information about the content they consume and ensure transparency throughout the content creation process.

User-Centric Design: The future holds promise for AI content creation tools that incorporate user-centric design principles. This means users will have more control over the AI generation process, allowing them to specify desired levels of transparency, bias mitigation techniques, and content attributes.

3. The Rise of AI as a Creative Partner

AI-Powered Brainstorming and Co-Creation: Imagine AI as a full-fledged creative partner, not just a content generation tool. Brainstorming sessions could be revolutionized by AI suggesting unique content ideas, exploring different creative angles, and even helping overcome writer's block in real-time.

AI-Driven Content Insights and Personalization: AI could analyze vast amounts of content performance data to provide personalized recommendations on content topics, formats, and styles that are likely to resonate best with your target audience. This will allow for the creation of highly targeted and impactful content strategies.

4. The Importance of Human-AI Collaboration

Human Oversight and Editorial Control: While AI capabilities continue to advance, human oversight and editorial control will remain paramount. Humans will continue to guide the AI with vision, strategic thinking, and critical analysis, ensuring the content aligns with brand voice, adheres to editorial standards, and achieves desired goals.

The Evolving Role of Human Content Creators: As AI takes over more of the heavy lifting, human content creators will likely focus on higher-level tasks like strategic content planning, audience engagement, and creative direction. This shift will allow human creators to leverage their unique strengths in storytelling, emotional intelligence, and brand understanding to create content that truly connects with audiences.

A Future of Responsible and Empowering AI

The future of AI and content creation is not about AI replacing human creators. Instead, it's about a powerful and mutually beneficial collaboration. By embracing AI as a tool to empower creativity, streamline workflows, and mitigate bias, we can usher in a new era of responsible and impactful content creation. This human-AI synergy will empower creators to produce high-quality, engaging content that resonates with their audience and achieves their content marketing goals.

Chapter 9

Staying Ahead of the Curve: Exploring Advanced Applications of Gemini AI

Congratulations! You've mastered the fundamentals of working with Gemini AI and unlocked its potential to revolutionize your content creation process. This chapter delves into advanced applications of Gemini AI, empowering you to push the boundaries of creativity and explore innovative ways to leverage this powerful tool.

9.1 Unforeseen Applications: Exploring New Frontiers with Gemini AI

While Chapter 9 explores advanced applications of Gemini AI, the true potential of this technology lies in venturing beyond the expected. This section dives into some unforeseen applications, encouraging you to push the boundaries and creatively leverage Gemini AI in uncharted territories of content creation.

9.1.1 Reimagining Interactive Content Experiences

AI-Driven Narrative Branching: Imagine using Gemini AI to create choose-your-own-adventure style content. The AI could generate different narrative branches based on user choices, providing an interactive and personalized storytelling experience.

AI-Powered Chatbots and Virtual Assistants: Gemini AI could be instrumental in developing chatbots and virtual assistants that can engage users in informative and conversational content experiences.

Interactive Content with Real-Time Adaptation: Consider content that adapts and evolves based on user interaction. Gemini AI could generate prompts or responses based on user input, creating a dynamic and engaging content experience.

9.1.2 Pushing the Boundaries of Content Formats

AI-Generated Scripts for Podcasts or Videos: Explore using Gemini AI to generate scripts for podcasts or video content. The AI could craft storylines, dialogue, or even video descriptions to streamline your content creation process.

AI-Powered Presentations and Slide Decks: Imagine using AI to generate compelling presentations or slide decks. Provide the AI with key information and it could create structured content with visually appealing layouts.

AI-Generated Social Media Content Calendars: Experiment with using Gemini AI to brainstorm social media content ideas and even generate draft posts tailored to different platforms and target audiences.

9.1.3 Rethinking Content Accessibility

AI-Generated Content in Multiple Languages: Gemini AI has the potential to break down language barriers. Explore its capabilities to generate content in multiple languages, increasing the reach of your content and promoting global accessibility.

AI-Powered Content for Different Reading Levels: Imagine using AI to personalize content difficulty to cater to different reading levels or age groups. This could be valuable for creating educational content or ensuring your content is inclusive for all audiences.

AI-Described Audio Content: Gemini AI could be instrumental in generating audio descriptions for visually-impaired audiences. This can make your content more inclusive and accessible to a wider range of users.

9.1.4 The Future of Unforeseen Applications

The potential applications of Gemini AI are constantly expanding. Here's a glimpse into what the future might hold:

AI-Composed Music or Soundscapes: Imagine AI generating original music or soundscapes to complement your content and enrich the user experience.

AI-Driven Content Gamification: The future could see AI being used to gamify content, making the consumption of information more interactive and engaging.

AI-Powered Content Summarization and Analysis: AI might condense lengthy content or generate summaries that highlight key takeaways, catering to users with limited time.

Embrace the Spirit of Exploration

Don't be afraid to experiment! Gemini AI is a powerful tool that can be adapted to your unique creative vision. As you explore these unforeseen applications and continuously test new ideas, you can become a pioneer in pushing the boundaries of content creation with AI.

The Takeaway: The Power is in Your Hands

The key to unlocking the true potential of Gemini AI lies in your imagination and willingness to explore. By thinking creatively and experimenting with unforeseen applications, you can leverage AI to transform your content creation process and deliver exceptional results that captivate your audience and propel your content marketing efforts to new heights.

9.2 The Evolving Landscape of AI Writing: Keeping Up with the Latest Developments

The realm of AI writing is a dynamic one, constantly evolving and pushing the boundaries of what's possible. Here's how to stay informed and ensure you're leveraging the most cutting-edge advancements in AI writing with Gemini AI and beyond:

1. Follow Industry Publications and Blogs

Stay Ahead of the Curve: Subscribe to publications and blogs that focus on AI, machine learning, and content creation. These resources will provide insights into the latest developments, research findings, and industry trends in AI writing.

Examples of Resources: Here are some potential resources to get you started:

Machine Learning Mastery Blog: https://machinelearningmastery.com/blog/ (https://machinelearningmastery.com/blog/)

VentureBeat: https://venturebeat.com/: AI and machine learning section

Towards Data Science: https://towardsdatascience.com/: AI and machine learning content

2. Attend Industry Events and Conferences

Immerse Yourself in the Community: Participating in industry events and conferences allows you to network with other AI enthusiasts, content creators, and developers. This fosters knowledge sharing and keeps you updated on the latest advancements and discussions surrounding AI writing.

Examples of Events: Here are some potential events to consider:

AAAI Conference on Artificial Intelligence (AAAI): https://annualmeeting.aaaai.org/

EMNLP: Conference on Empirical Methods in Natural Language Processing: https://2023.emnlp.org/

Content Marketing World: https://contentmarketingworld.com/ (tracks might cover AI in content creation)

3. Explore Online Courses and Tutorials

Deepen Your Understanding: Consider enrolling in online courses or tutorials offered by reputable platforms like Coursera, Udacity, or Udemy. These courses can provide a more in-depth understanding of AI writing fundamentals, along with exploring the latest advancements and applications.

Course Examples: Here are some potential starting points:

Natural Language Processing Specialization: https://www.coursera.org/specializations/natural-language-processing by deeplearning.ai on Coursera

Introduction to Artificial Intelligence: [invalid URL removed] by Udacity

AI Content Writing Masterclass: [invalid URL removed] (specific course to explore)

4. Experiment with Beta Testing New Features

Be an Early Adopter: Many AI writing tools, including Gemini AI, might offer beta testing opportunities for new features. Participating in beta testing allows you to get hands-on experience with cutting-edge functionalities and provide valuable feedback to help shape the future of AI writing technology.

Stay Updated with Gemini AI: Keep an eye out for announcements from Gemini AI regarding beta testing opportunities or new feature rollouts.

5. Engage with the AI Writing Community

Connect and Share Knowledge: Online forums, communities, and social media groups dedicated to AI writing can be valuable resources. Engage in discussions, ask questions, and share your experiences to learn from others and stay informed about the latest trends.

Examples of Communities: Here are some online communities to explore:

Reddit's r/artificial https://www.reddit.com/r/artificial/

Facebook groups focused on AI content creation or content marketing

LinkedIn groups on AI or machine learning

The Future of AI Writing is Here

By staying informed and actively engaging with the evolving landscape of AI writing, you can ensure you're utilizing the most advanced features and functionalities. This will empower you to create high-quality, engaging content that stands out in today's competitive digital landscape. Remember, AI is a powerful tool, and with continuous learning and exploration, you can become a master of leveraging AI writing to achieve remarkable results.

9.3 Future-Proofing Your Skills: Adapting to the Changing Content Landscape

The content creation landscape is undergoing a significant transformation with the rise of AI writing tools like Gemini AI. While AI automates certain tasks, it won't replace human content creators. The key to success lies in adapting your skillset to complement and collaborate effectively with AI. Here's how to future-proof your skills and thrive in this evolving environment:

9.3.1 Developing Your Strategic Thinking Skills

Shifting Focus from Craft to Strategy: As AI handles content generation, human content creators will need to focus more on strategic planning. This involves developing a deep understanding of your target audience, identifying content gaps, and creating data-driven content strategies that align with your overall marketing goals.

Content Ideation and Brainstorming: AI can assist with content generation, but human creativity remains irreplaceable. Sharpen your brainstorming skills to develop unique content ideas that captivate your audience and set you apart from the competition.

Content Curation and Editorial Control: The ability to curate high-quality content from various sources and exercise editorial control to ensure brand alignment and quality will remain paramount in the age of AI.

9.3.2 Refining Your Editing and Proofreading Skills

Human Touch in Editing and Revision: Even AI-generated content requires human editing to ensure flawless grammar, cohesive structure, and adherence to your brand voice and style. Refine your editing and proofreading skills to maintain the polish and professionalism of your content.

Fact-Checking and Verification: The responsibility of fact-checking and verifying information ultimately lies with human creators. As AI content continues to evolve, critical thinking and the ability to discern factual accuracy will be essential.

9.3.3 Mastering the Art of Storytelling

The Power of Compelling Narratives: In a world saturated with content, compelling storytelling is what will truly resonate with your audience. Hone your storytelling skills to craft narratives that capture attention, evoke emotions, and leave a lasting impression.

Content Personalization and Targeting: The ability to tailor content to specific audience segments and personalize the user experience will be crucial for success. Develop your skills in content personalization to create content that genuinely connects with your target audience.

9.3.4 Embracing New Technologies and Tools

Staying Ahead of the Curve: The world of AI is constantly evolving. Demonstrate a willingness to learn about new AI writing tools and explore how they can augment your content creation process.

Becoming an AI-Savvy Content Creator: The future belongs to those who can effectively collaborate with AI. Strive to become an AI-savvy content creator who can leverage the power of AI while maintaining human creativity and strategic thinking at the forefront.

The Future of Content Creation is a Human-AI Partnership

The rise of AI writing tools doesn't signal the end of human content creators. Instead, it's a call to evolve and adapt. By developing the skills highlighted above, you can position yourself as a valuable asset in the content creation landscape. Embrace AI as a collaborator, and focus on the strategic thinking, storytelling, and human touch that AI cannot replicate. This human-AI partnership will be the key to unlocking unprecedented content creation success in the years to come.

Chapter 10

The Final Word: Mastering Gemini AI and Owning Your Content Creation Journey

Congratulations! You've reached the final chapter of this comprehensive guide to Gemini AI. Throughout this journey, you've explored the potential of this powerful tool and acquired the knowledge to transform your content creation process.

Key Takeaways

Gemini AI: Your Partner in Content Creation: Gemini AI is more than just a content generation tool. It's a valuable partner that can streamline workflows, spark creative ideas, and elevate the quality of your content.

The Power is in Your Hands: The key to unlocking the true potential of Gemini AI lies in your creativity and strategic vision. By providing clear prompts, utilizing advanced functionalities, and focusing on human-centric storytelling, you can generate exceptional content that resonates with your audience.

The Future of Content Creation: The content creation landscape is constantly evolving, and AI is here to stay. By embracing AI and developing the complementary skillset outlined in this guide, you can future-proof your content creation career and thrive in this exciting new era.

Owning Your Content Creation Journey

As you move forward with Gemini AI, remember **you are the author of your content creation journey**. While AI can be a powerful tool, the human element remains paramount. Your strategic thinking, creative vision, and editorial control will distinguish your content and set you apart from the competition.

Here are some final words of encouragement:

Embrace Experimentation: Don't be afraid to experiment with different functionalities and explore new ways to leverage Gemini AI. The more you experiment, the more you'll discover its potential and unleash its capabilities within your workflow.

Focus on Quality and Value: While AI can generate content quickly, never compromise on quality. Always prioritize creating valuable content that informs, engages, and inspires your audience.

Maintain Your Creative Spark: AI is a powerful tool, but it cannot replace human creativity. Continue to nurture your creativity, explore new ideas, and find ways to infuse your unique voice into your content.

The Future is Bright

The world of content creation is brimming with exciting possibilities. With Gemini AI by your side and the human touch leading the way, you have the power to craft remarkable content that stands out, connects with your audience, and achieves your content marketing goals.

We wish you all the best on your content creation journey!

10:1 The Final Word: Mastering Gemini AI and Owning Your Content Creation Journey:

Key Takeaways

Gemini AI as a Partner: Gemini AI is more than just a content generation tool. It's a valuable collaborator that streamlines workflows, sparks creative ideas, and elevates content quality.

The Power Lies with You: Effective use of Gemini AI requires your creativity, strategic vision, clear prompts, and human-centric storytelling.

The Future of Content Creation: The landscape is ever-changing, and AI is here to stay. Embrace AI and develop complementary skills to thrive.

Owning Your Content Creation Journey

You are the Author: While AI is a powerful tool, you are ultimately the author of your content creation journey. Your strategic thinking, creative vision, and editorial control set you apart.

Final Words of Encouragement

Experiment: Don't be afraid to experiment with different functionalities and explore new ways to leverage Gemini AI.

Focus on Quality and Value: Always prioritize creating informative, engaging, and inspiring content.

Maintain Your Creative Spark: Nurture your creativity, explore new ideas, and infuse your unique voice into your content.

The Future is Bright

With Gemini AI by your side and the human touch leading the way, you have the power to craft remarkable content that achieves your content marketing goals.

Essential Skills (These are not explicitly stated in Chapter 10, but can be inferred throughout the book)

Understanding of AI Content Creation: Familiarity with how AI generates content and its limitations.

Prompt Engineering: The ability to craft effective prompts that guide Gemini AI in the desired direction.

Content Editing and Proofreading: Skills to ensure grammatical accuracy, cohesive structure, and brand alignment.

Content Strategy: The ability to develop data-driven content plans that align with marketing goals.

Storytelling: The ability to craft compelling narratives that capture attention and resonate with your audience.

Critical Thinking: The ability to evaluate information and discern factual accuracy, especially with AI-generated content.

Staying Current with AI Developments: A willingness to learn about new AI writing tools and explore their applications.

10.2 Common Challenges and How to Overcome Them: Troubleshooting Your Gemini AI Experience

Even the most powerful tools can encounter occasional hiccups. Here are some common challenges you might face while using Gemini AI, along with solutions to get you back on track:

Challenge 1: Unsatisfactory Content Generation

Possible Cause: Your prompts might be unclear, lacking sufficient detail, or not specific enough regarding content style or target audience.

Solution: Refine your prompts. Provide more context, specify the desired tone and style, and include target audience information. Use the advanced prompt techniques covered in Chapter 9.1 for even more control.

Challenge 2: Factual Inaccuracy or Bias in Generated Content

Possible Cause: The training data used by Gemini AI might contain biases, or your prompts might inadvertently lead the AI in a biased direction.

Solution: Fact-check all AI-generated content, especially for sensitive topics. Review your prompts for any potential bias and revise them to ensure neutrality. Explore using fairness tools mentioned in Chapter 8.2 to mitigate bias in your content generation process.

Challenge 3: Technical Glitches or Downtime

Possible Cause: Temporary technical issues on the Gemini AI platform.

Solution: Try refreshing the page or restarting your device. If the issue persists, check the Gemini AI website or social media channels for any service outage announcements.

Challenge 4: Difficulty Brainstorming New Content Ideas

Possible Cause: Feeling stuck in a creative rut.

Solution: Gemini AI can be your brainstorming partner! Use its capabilities explored in Chapter 9.1 to generate content ideas based on broad keywords or themes.

Challenge 5: Integrating Gemini AI with Your Existing Workflow

Possible Cause: Unsure how to seamlessly integrate AI-generated content into your existing workflow.

Solution: Explore potential integrations mentioned in Chapter 9.4. If there's no current integration for your specific tool, consider exporting your AI-generated content and importing it manually.

Remember, these are just a few common challenges. If you encounter an issue not listed here, don't hesitate to consult the Gemini AI Help Center or reach out to their support team.

Additional Tips for Troubleshooting

Start Simple: When starting with Gemini AI, begin with simple prompts and gradually increase complexity as you gain experience.

Proofread and Edit Thoroughly: Always edit and proofread AI-generated content to ensure accuracy, adherence to your brand voice, and overall quality.

Provide Feedback: If you encounter consistent issues or have suggestions for improvement, provide feedback to the Gemini AI team. Your input can help them continuously improve the tool.

By following these tips and understanding common challenges, you can troubleshoot your Gemini AI experience and unlock its full potential to transform your content creation process.

10.3 Looking Forward: The Power of AI in Shaping the Future of Content

The future of content creation is undeniably intertwined with the ever-evolving world of AI. As AI capabilities continue to advance, we can expect to see significant transformations in how content is created, distributed, and consumed. Here's a glimpse into what the future holds:

AI-Driven Content Personalization at Scale

Imagine a world where content adapts and personalizes itself in real-time based on individual user preferences and behavior. AI could analyze user data to tailor content delivery, suggest relevant information, and personalize the user experience to a whole new level.

The Rise of AI-Powered Content Curation

Content curation involves gathering information from various sources and presenting it in a cohesive and informative way. AI can excel at curating content by identifying the most relevant and valuable pieces based on user needs and interests.

Democratization of Content Creation with AI

In the future, AI might make high-quality content creation more accessible to everyone. User-friendly AI tools could empower anyone to generate drafts, brainstorm ideas, or translate content into different languages, even without extensive writing experience.

The Evolving Role of Human Content Creators

As AI takes over more of the content generation heavy lifting, human content creators will likely focus on higher-level tasks like strategic content planning, managing editorial workflows, and overseeing the creative vision. Human expertise in storytelling, emotional intelligence, and brand understanding will remain paramount in the age of AI.

The Importance of Responsible AI Development

As AI continues to shape the content creation landscape, it's crucial to ensure responsible AI development practices are upheld. This involves mitigating bias, promoting transparency, and prioritizing the ethical use of AI in content creation.

A Future of Human-AI Collaboration

The future of content creation is not about AI replacing human creators. Instead, it's about collaboration. By leveraging AI as a powerful tool and combining it with human creativity and strategic thinking, we can usher in a new era of content creation that is informative, engaging, and truly impactful.

The Final Word: Embracing the Potential

The potential of AI in shaping the future of content is vast and exciting. By embracing AI and continuously learning about its capabilities, you can position yourself at the forefront of this dynamic content creation landscape. As AI continues to evolve, the possibilities are limitless. So, get ready to write the next chapter in the ever-evolving story of content creation!

www.ingramcontent.com/pod-product-compliance
Lightning Source LLC
LaVergne TN
LVHW051740050326
832903LV00023B/1020